HENRY LAWSON
Favourite Poems

W. HATHEREL

HENRY LAWSON
Favourite Poems

Illustrated with Australian Landscape Paintings

Selected by Margaret Olds

Sydney
THE CARMEL PRESS

Published by
The Carmel Press
an imprint of Murray Child & Company Pty Ltd
64 Suffolk Avenue, Collaroy Plateau, NSW, Australia, 2098
First Edition 1992
This collection of poems and paintings
© Murray Child & Company Pty Ltd 1992
© Design Murray Child & Company Pty Ltd, 1992
This book has been edited, designed, typeset and electronically
composed in Australia by the publisher
Typesetting processed by Deblaere Typesetting Pty Ltd
Printed in Singapore by Colourwork Press Pte Ltd

National Library of Australia
Cataloguing-in-Publication data

Lawson, Henry, 1867–1922.
Henry Lawson favourite poems.

ISBN 0 908048 11 4.

I. Olds, Margaret. II. Title. III. Title: Favourite poems.

A821.2

Contents

Introduction   6

Andy's Gone with Cattle   8

Taking His Chance   10

The Great Grey Plain   12

Song of the Old Bullock-Driver   16

The Song and the Sigh   18

The Blue Mountains   20

The Heart of the Swag   22

Somewhere Up in Queensland   24

The Ballad of the Drover   26

Reedy River   30

Faces in the Street   33

To an Old Mate   37

The Shearers   40

The Bush Fire   42

The Old Bark School   46

Introduction

Henry Lawson was born on the goldfields at Grenfell, NSW, on 17 June 1867. His father, Niels Hertzberg Larsen, later known as Peter Lawson, was a Norwegian sailor who had jumped ship in Melbourne to seek his fortune on the goldfields. His mother, Louisa, was born and educated near the New South Wales town of Mudgee where she showed early signs of her developing interest in women's issues and radicalism.

Soon after Henry's birth, the family returned to Eurunderee, near Mudgee, where Peter Lawson had earlier taken up land. Henry was nine years old when the first school opened at Eurunderee (immortalised in "The Old Bark School") and the deafness which was to burden him all his life became apparent about this time. He left school at the age of thirteen to work with his father building houses in the area.

In 1883 his parents separated and Louisa moved to Sydney. Shortly afterwards, Louisa sent for Henry and apprenticed him as a coach-painter at the carriage-building firm of Hudson Brothers at Clyde. At home with Louisa, he met her many radical friends and became interested in social reform and the republican movement.

In 1887 Louisa bought the *Republican* newspaper and Lawson's first prose piece was published there in that same year. Also in 1887 Lawson's first poem, "A Song of the Republic", was published in the *Bulletin*. In 1888 "Faces in the Street", a moving poem about the social injustices of the times, was published in the *Bulletin* and Lawson became famous almost overnight.

From 1888 to 1892, Lawson's talent blossomed and his reputation as a poet and a short story writer was established. However the financial rewards were not great. About 1890 he embarked on a journalistic career and travelled much of Australia looking for work. Despite his early success, by 1892 Lawson was feeling depressed about his life and work and was already addicted to alcohol.

In 1892–93 J. F. Archibald, editor of the *Bulletin*, sent Lawson to Bourke to report on the great drought. As part of the trip he tramped from Bourke to Hungerford and back. This period gave Lawson an added insight into the harshness of life in the bush and the outback characters and provided him with much material for his poems and short stories.

Short Stories in Prose and Verse was published by Lawson and his mother in 1894. Then in 1896 *In the Days When the World Was Wide* and *While the Billy Boils* were published by Angus & Robertson. Both books were very well received. At this period Lawson was at the height of his powers and, in that same year, he married Bertha Bredt. They moved to Western Australia and then to New Zealand, hoping a change of scene would help with his drinking problem. In 1898 the Lawsons returned to Sydney but before the end of the year Lawson experienced his first hospitalisation in a clinic for inebriates.

In 1900 the Lawsons moved to London, in an attempt to start a new life. At first, Lawson was successsful; he received encouragement from the critics and was published in the leading journals. However, feelings of isolation and loneliness took their toll and he started drinking heavily again. In 1902 the Lawsons again returned to Sydney and in 1903, Bertha, unable to cope any longer, separated from Lawson.

From this time on, Lawson's deterioration became more and more obvious. Both his health and his work suffered, with his poems and stories showing only occasional flashes of his earlier brilliance. Over the following years he depended on the generosity of his friends and, finally, on a small literary pension from the Federal Government for his income. In his last years he relied heavily on his "little landlady", Mrs Byers, and died at her cottage at Abbotsford on 2 September 1922. He was given a State funeral and buried at Waverley cemetery.

Despite his personal problems Henry Lawson made a unique contribution to Australian literature. His poems and stories captured the lives of ordinary Australians, both in the city and in the bush, and have helped to shape the Australian ethos and the way we see ourselves today. "The Ballad of the Drover", "Faces in the Street" and "The Bush Fire" are as valid and moving today as they were when they were written.

Some of Australia's best loved paintings have been chosen to accompany this selection. From the brushes of such well-known artists as Frederick McCubbin, Tom Roberts, Walter Withers and Frank Mahoney, these paintings from the time of Lawson complement the poems and will give the reader new insight into them. The poems and paintings together reflect the lives of our forebears and show how they worked, lived and played.

Margaret Olds

Andy's Gone with Cattle

Our Andy's gone to battle now
   'Gainst Drought, the red marauder;
Our Andy's gone with cattle now
   Across the Queensland border.

He's left us in dejection now;
   Our hearts with him are roving.
It's dull on this selection now,
   Since Andy went a-droving.

Who now shall wear the cheerful face
   In times when things are slackest?
And who shall whistle round the place
   When Fortune frowns her blackest?

Oh, who shall cheek the squatter now
   When he comes round us snarling?
His tongue is growing hotter now
   Since Andy cross'd the Darling.

The gates are out of order now,
   In storms the "riders" rattle;
For far across the border now
   Our Andy's gone with cattle.

Poor Aunty's looking thin and white;
   And Uncle's cross with worry;
And poor old Blucher howls all night
   Since Andy left Macquarie.

Frank Mahoney, Australia, 1862–1917, *Rounding up a straggler*, 1889, oil on canvas 91.5 x
127.6 cm. Art Gallery of New South Wales. Purchased 1889.

Oh, may the showers in torrents fall,
    And all the tanks run over;
And may the grass grow green and tall
    In pathways of the drover;

And may good angels send the rain
    On desert stretches sandy;
And when the summer comes again
    God grant 'twill bring us Andy.

Taking His Chance

They stood by the door of the Inn on the Rise;
May Carney looked up in the bushranger's eyes:
"Oh! why did you come?—it was mad of you, Jack;
You know that the troopers are out on your track."
A laugh and a shake of his obstinate head—
"I wanted a dance, and I'll chance it," he said.

Some twenty-odd bushmen had come to the "ball",
But Jack from his youth had been known to them all,
And bushmen are soft where a woman is fair,
So the love of May Carney protected him there;
And all the short evening—it seems like romance—
She danced with a bushranger taking his chance.

'Twas midnight—the dancers stood suddenly still,
For hoofs had been heard on the side of the hill!
Ben Duggan, the drover, along the hillside
Came riding as only a bushman can ride.
He sprang from his horse, to the shanty he sped—
"The troopers are down in the gully!" he said.

Quite close to the homestead the troopers were seen.
"Clear out and ride hard for the ranges, Jack Dean!
Be quick!" said May Carney—her hand on her heart—
"We'll bluff them awhile, and 'twill give you a start."
He lingered a moment—to kiss her, of course—
Then ran to the trees where he'd hobbled his horse.

She ran to the gate, and the troopers were there—
The jingle of hobbles came faint on the air—
Then loudly she screamed; it was only to drown

Patrick William Maroney, *Police riding through gully*, ca 1894, oil on canvas 107 x 61 cm.
National Library of Australia.

The treacherous clatter of slip-rails let down.
But troopers are sharp, and they saw at a glance
That someone was taking a desperate chance.

They chased, and they shouted, "Surrender, Jack Dean!"
They called him three times in the name of the Queen.
Then came from the darkness the clicking of locks;
The crack of the rifles was heard in the rocks!
A shriek and a shout, and a rush of pale men—
And there lay the bushranger, chancing it then.

The sergeant dismounted and knelt on the sod—
"Your bushranging's over—make peace, Jack, with God!"
The bushranger laughed—not a word he replied,
But turned to the girl who knelt down by his side.
He gazed in her eyes as she lifted his head:
"Just kiss me—my girl—and—I'll—chance it," he said.

The Great Grey Plain

Out West, where the stars are brightest,
    Where the scorching north wind blows,
And the bones of the dead gleam whitest,
    And the sun on a desert glows—
Yet within the selfish kingdom
    Where man starves man for gain,
Where white men tramp for existence—
    Wide lies the Great Grey Plain.

David Davies, 1864–1939, Australian, *Moonrise*, 1894, oil on canvas 119.8 x 150 cm. Purchased 1895. National Gallery of Victoria.

No break in its awful horizon,
    No blur in the dazzling haze,
Save where by the bordering timber
    The fierce, white heat-waves blaze,
And out where the tank-heap rises
    Or looms when the sunlights wane,
Till it seems like a distant mountain
    Low down on the Great Grey Plain.

No sign of a stream or fountain,
    No spring on its dry, hot breast,

No shade from the blazing noontide
    Where a weary man might rest.
Whole years go by when the glowing
    Sky never clouds for rain—
Only the shrubs of the desert
    Grow on the Great Grey Plain.

From the camp, while the rich man's dreaming,
    Come the "traveller" and his mate,
In the ghastly daybreak seeming
    Like a swagman's ghost out late;
And the horseman blurs in the distance,
    While still the stars remain,
A low, faint dust-cloud haunting
    His track on the Great Grey Plain.

And all day long from before them
    The mirage smokes away—
That daylight ghost of an ocean
    Creeps close behind all day
With an evil, snake-like motion,
    As the waves of a madman's brain:
'Tis a phantom *not* like water
    Out there on the Great Grey Plain.

There's a run on the Western limit
    Where a man lives like a beast;
And a shanty in the mulga
    That stretches to the East;
And the hopeless men who carry
    Their swags and tramp in pain—
The footmen must not tarry
    Out there on the Great Grey Plain.

Out West, where the stars are brightest,
　　Where the scorching north wind blows,
And the bones of the dead seem whitest,
　　And the sun on a desert glows—
Out back in the hungry distance
　　That brave hearts dare in vain—
Where beggars tramp for existence—
　　There lies the Great Grey Plain.

'Tis a desert not more barren
　　Than the Great Grey Plain of years,
Where a fierce fire burns the hearts of men—
　　Dries up the fount of tears;
Where the victims of a greed insane
　　Are crushed in a hell-born strife—
Where the souls of a race are murdered
　　On the Great Grey Plain of Life.

Song of the Old Bullock-Driver

Far back in the days when the blacks used to ramble
    In long single file 'neath the evergreen tree,
The wool-teams in season came down from Coonamble,
    And journeyed for weeks on their way to the sea.
'Twas then that our hearts and our sinews were stronger,
    For those were the days when the bushman was bred.
We journeyed on roads that were rougher and longer
    Than roads where the feet of our grandchildren tread.

With mates who have gone to the great Never-Never,
    And mates whom I've not seen for many a day,
I camped on the banks of the Cudgegong River
    And yarned at the fire by the old bullock-dray.
I would summon them back from the far Riverina,
    From days that shall be from all others distinct,
And sing to the sound of an old concertina
    Their rugged old songs where strange fancies were linked.

We never were lonely, for, camping together,
    We yarned and we smoked the long evenings away,
And little I cared for the signs of the weather
    When snug in my hammock slung under the dray.
We rose with the dawn, were it ever so chilly,
    When yokes and tarpaulins were covered with frost
And toasted the bacon and boiled the black billy,
    Where high on the camp-fire the branches were tossed.

On flats where the air was suggestive of possums,
    And homesteads and fences were hinting of change,
We saw the faint glimmer of appletree blossoms,
    And far in the distance the blue of the range;

And here in the rain, there was small use in flogging
    The poor, tortured bullocks that tugged at the load,
When down to the axles the waggons were bogging
    And traffic was making a marsh of the road.

'Twas hard on the beasts on the terrible pinches,
    Where two teams of bullocks were yoked to a load,
And tugging and slipping, and moving by inches,
    Half-way to the summit they clung to the road.
And then, when the last of the pinches was bested,
    (You'll surely not say that a glass was a sin?)
The bullocks lay down 'neath the gum trees and rested—
    The bullockies steered for the bar of the inn.

Then slowly we crawled by the trees that kept tally
    Of miles that were passed on the long journey down.

David Davies, 1864–1939, Australian, *A hot day*, 1888, oil on canvas 60.6 x 91.3 cm. Felton Bequest 1937, National Gallery of Victoria.

We saw the wild beauty of Capertee Valley,
  As slowly we rounded the base of the Crown.
But, ah! the poor bullocks were cruelly goaded
  While climbing the hills from the flats and the vales;
'Twas here that the teams were so often unloaded
  That all knew the meaning of "counting your bales".

And, oh! but the best-paying load that I carried
  Was one to the run where my sweetheart was nurse.
We courted awhile, and agreed to get married,
  And couple our futures for better or worse.
And as my old feet grew too weary to drag on
  The miles of rough metal they met by the way,
My eldest grew up and I gave him the waggon—
  He's plodding along by the bullocks to-day.

The Song and the Sigh

The creek went down with a broken song,
  'Neath the sheoaks high;
The waters carried the tune along,
  And the oaks a sigh.

The song and the sigh went winding by,
  Went winding down;
Circling the foot of the mountain high,
  And the hillside brown.

A. Henry Fullwood, Australia, 1863–1930, *The station boundary*, 1891, oil on canvas 61.6 x 92 cm.
Art Gallery of New South Wales. Purchased 1891.

They were hushed in the swamp of the Dead Man's Crime,
  Where the curlews cried;
But they reached the river the self same time,
  And there they died.

And the creek of life goes winding on,
  Wandering by;
And bears for ever, its course upon,
  A song and a sigh.

The Blue Mountains

Above the ashes straight and tall,
  Through ferns with moisture dripping,
I climb beneath the sandstone wall,
  My feet on mosses slipping.

Like ramparts round the valley's edge
  The tinted cliffs are standing,

A. Henry Fullwood, 1863–1930, *Echo Point,* ca 1904, oil on paper 16 x 32.2 cm. National Library of Australia.

With many a broken wall and ledge,
    And many a rocky landing.

And round about their rugged feet
    Deep ferny dells are hidden
In shadowed depths, whence dust and heat
    Are banished and forbidden.

The stream that, crooning to itself,
    Comes down a tireless rover,
Flows calmly to the rocky shelf,
    And there leaps bravely over.

Now pouring down, now lost in spray
    When mountain breezes sally,
The water strikes the rock midway,
    And leaps into the valley.

*   *   *

Now in the west the colours change,
    The blue with crimson blending;
Behind the far Dividing Range
    The sun is fast descending.

And mellowed day comes o'er the place,
    And softens ragged edges;
The rising moon's great placid face
    Looks gravely o'er the ledges.

The Heart of the Swag

Oh! the track through the scrub groweth ever more dreary,
    And lower and lower his grey head doth bow;
For the swagman is old and the swagman is weary—
    He's been tramping for over a century now.
He tramps in a worn-out old "side spring" and "blucher",
    His hat is a ruin, his coat is a rag,
And he carries for ever, far into the future,
    The key of his life in the core of his swag.

There are old-fashioned portraits of girls who are grannies,
    There are tresses of dark hair whose owners are grey;
There are faded old letters from Marys and Annies,
    And Toms, Dicks, and Harrys, dead many a day.
There are broken-heart secrets and bitter-heart reasons—
    They are sewn in a canvas or calico bag,

Frederick McCubbin, *Down on his luck*, oil on canvas 114.5 x 152.8 cm. Collection, Art Gallery of Western Australia.

And wrapped up in oilskin through dark rainy seasons,
    And he carries them safe in the core of his swag.

There are letters that should have been burnt in the past time,
    For he reads them alone, and a devil it brings;
There were farewells that should have been said for the last time,
    For, for ever and ever the love for her springs.
But he keeps them all precious, and keeps them in order,
    And no matter to man how his footsteps may drag,
There's a friend who will find, when he crosses the Border,
    That the Heart of the Man's in the Heart of his Swag.

Somewhere Up in Queensland

He's somewhere up in Queensland,
    The old folks used to say;
He's somewhere up in Queensland,
    The people say to-day.
But Somewhere (up in Queensland)
    That uncle used to know—
That filled our hearts with wonder,
    Seems vanished long ago.

He's gone to Queensland, droving,
    The old folks used to say;
He's gone to Queensland, droving,
    The people say to-day.
But "gone to Queensland, droving",
    Might mean in language plain,
He follows stock in buggies,
    And gets supplies by train.

He's knocking round in Queensland,
    The old folks used to say;
He's gone to Queensland, roving,
    His sweetheart says to-day.
But "gone to Queensland, roving"
    By mighty plain and scrub,
Might mean he drives a motor-car
    For Missus Moneygrub.

He's looking for new country,
    The old folks used to say;
Our boy has gone exploring,
    Fond parents say to-day.

"Exploring" out in Queensland
   Might only mean to some
He's salesman in "the drapery"
   Of a bush emporium.

To Somewhere up in Queensland
   Went Tom and Ted and Jack;
From Somewhere up in Queensland
   The dusty cheques come back:
From Somewhere up in Queensland
   Brown drovers used to come,
And Someone up in Queensland
   Kept many a southern home.

Somewhere up in Queensland,
   How many black sheep roam,
Who never write a letter,
   And never think of home.
For Someone up in Queensland
   How many a mother spoke;
For Someone up in Queensland
   How many a girl's heart broke.

John Ford Paterson, Australia, 1851–1912, *Nearing the camping ground* ,1889, oil on canvas 122.5 x 199.3 cm. Art Gallery of New South Wales. Purchased 1890.

The Ballad of the Drover

Across the stony ridges,
  Across the rolling plain,
Young Harry Dale, the drover,
  Comes riding home again.
And well his stock-horse bears him,
  And light of heart is he,
And stoutly his old pack-horse
  Is trotting by his knee.

Up Queensland way with cattle
  He's travelled regions vast;
And many months have vanished
  Since home-folks saw him last.
He hums a song of someone
  He hopes to marry soon;
And hobble-chains and camp-ware
  Keep jingling to the tune.

Beyond the hazy dado
  Against the lower skies
And yon blue line of ranges
  The station homestead lies.
And thitherward the drover
  Jogs through the lazy noon,
While hobble-chains and camp-ware
  All jingling to a tune.

An hour has filled the heavens
  With storm-clouds inky black;
At times the lightning trickles
  Around the drover's track;

Tom Roberts, Australia, 1856–1931, *In a corner of the Macintyre*, 1895, oil on canvas 71.7 x 86.4 cm. Collection: Australian National Gallery.

But Harry pushes onward,
   His horses' strength he tries,
In hope to reach the river
   Before the flood shall rise.

The thunder from above him,
   Goes rolling o'er the plain;
And down on thirsty pastures
   In torrents falls the rain;
And every creek and gully
   Sends forth its little flood,
Till the river runs a banker,
   All stained with yellow mud.

Now Harry speaks to Rover,
    The best dog on the plains,
And to his hardy horses,
    And strokes their shaggy manes;
"We've breasted bigger rivers
    When floods were at their height,
Nor shall this gutter stop us
    From getting home tonight!"

The thunder growls a warning
    The ghastly lightnings gleam;
The drover turns his horses
    To swim the fatal stream.
But, oh! the flood runs stronger
    Than e'er it ran before;
The saddle-horse is failing,
    And only half-way o'er!

When flashes next the lightning,
    The flood's grey breast is blank;
A cattle dog and pack-horse
    Are struggling up the bank.
But in the lonely homestead
    The girl will wait in vain—
He'll never pass the stations
    In charge of stock again.

The faithful dog a moment
    Sits panting on the bank,
And then swims through the current
    To where his master sank.
And round and round in circles
    He fights with failing strength,

Till, borne down by the waters,
    The old dog sinks at length.
Across the flooded lowlands
    And slopes of sodden loam
The pack-horse struggles onward,
    To take dumb tidings home.
And mud-stained, wet, and weary,
    Through ranges dark goes he;
While hobble-chains and tinware
    Are sounding eerily.

The floods are in the ocean,
    The stream is clear again,
And now a verdant carpet
    Is stretched across the plain.
But someone's eyes are saddened,
    And someone's heart still bleeds
In sorrow for the drover
    Who sleeps among the reeds.

Reedy River

Ten miles down Reedy River
    A pool of water lies,
And all the year it mirrors
    The changes in the skies,
Within that pool's broad bosom
    Is room for all the stars;
It's bed of sand has drifted
    O'er countless rocky bars.

Around the lower edges
    There waves a bed of reeds,
Where water rats are hidden
    And where the wild duck breeds;
And grassy slopes rise gently
    To ridges long and low,
Where groves of wattle flourish
    And native bluebells grow.

Beneath the granite ridges
    The eye may just discern
Where Rocky Creek emerges
    From deep green banks of fern;
And standing tall between them,
    The drooping she-oaks cool
The hard, blue-tinted waters
    Before they reach the pool.

Ten miles down Reedy River
    One Sunday afternoon,
I rode with Mary Campbell
    To that broad, bright lagoon;

Frederick McCubbin, *A bush burial*, oil on canvas 122.5 x 224.5 cm. Signed and dated l.r., black paint, "F. McCubbin." Collection Geelong Art Gallery. Purchased by public subscription, 1900.

We left our horses grazing
    Till shadows climbed the peak,
And strolled beneath the she-oaks
    On the banks of Rocky Creek.

Then home along the river
    That night we rode a race,
And the moonlight lent a glory
    To Mary Campbell's face;
I pleaded for my future
    All thro' that moonlight ride,

Until our weary horses
    Drew closer side by side.

Ten miles from Ryan's Crossing
    And five below the peak,
I built a little homestead
    On the banks of Rocky Creek;
I cleared the land and fenced it
    And ploughed the rich red loam,
And my first crop was golden
    When I brought Mary home.

Now still down Reedy River
    The grassy she-oaks sigh;
The waterholes still mirror
    The pictures in the sky;
While the golden sand is drifting
    Across the rocky bars;
And over all for ever
    Go sun and moon and stars.

But of the hut I builded
    There are no traces now,
And many rains have levelled
    The furrows of my plough.
The glad bright days have vanished;
    For sombre branches wave
Their wattle-blossom golden
    Above my Mary's grave.

Faces in the Street

They lie, the men who tell us for reasons of their own,
That want is here a stranger, and that misery's unknown;
For where the nearest suburb and the city proper meet
My window-sill is level with the faces in the street—
 Drifting past, drifting past,
  To the beat of weary feet—
While I sorrow for the owners of those faces in the street.

And cause I have to sorrow, in a land so young and fair,
To see upon those faces stamped the marks of Want and Care;
I look in vain for traces of the fresh and fair and sweet
In sallow, sunken faces that are drifting through the street—
 Drifting on, drifting on,
  To the scrape of restless feet;
I can sorrow for the owners of the faces in the street.

In hours before the dawning dims the starlight in the sky
The wan and weary faces first begin to trickle by,
Increasing as the moments hurry on with morning feet,
Till like a pallid river flow the faces in the street—
 Flowing in, flowing in,
  To the beat of hurried feet—
Ah! I sorrow for the owners of those faces in the street.

The human river dwindles when 'tis past the hour of eight,
Its waves go flowing faster in the fear of being late;
But slowly drag the moments, whilst beneath the dust and heat
The city grinds the owners of the faces in the street—
 Grinding body, grinding soul,
  Yielding scarce enough to eat—
Oh! I sorrow for the owners of the faces in the street.

And then the only faces till the sun is sinking down
Are those of outside toilers and the idlers of the town,
Save here and there a face that seems a stranger in the street
Tells of the city's unemployed upon his weary beat—
    Drifting round, drifting round,
    To the tread of listless feet—
Ah! my heart aches for the owner of that sad face in the street.

And when the hours on lagging feet have slowly dragged away,
And sickly yellow gaslights rise to mock the going day,
Then, flowing past my window, like a tide in its retreat,
Again I see the pallid stream of faces in the street—
    Ebbing out, ebbing out,
    To the drag of tired feet,
While my heart is aching dumbly for the faces in the street.

And now all blurred and smirched with vice the day's sad pages
end,
For while the short "large hours" towards the longer "small hours"
trend,
With smiles that mock the wearer, and with words that half
entreat,
Delilah pleads for custom at the corner of the street—
    Sinking down, sinking down,
    Battered wreck by tempests beat—
A dreadful, thankless trade is hers, that Woman of the Street.

But, ah! to dreader things than these our fair young city comes,
For in its heart are growing thick the filthy dens and slums,
Where human forms shall rot away in sties for swine unmeet,
And ghostly faces shall be seen unfit for any street—
    Rotting out, rotting out,
    For the lack of air and meat—
In dens of vice and horror that are hidden from the street.

Giralamo Nerli, *A wet evening*, 1888, oil on canvas 32.2 x 40.3 cm. Gift of Howard Hinton, 1935.
The Howard Hinton Collection, New England Regional Art Museum, Armidale, NSW.

I wonder would the apathy of wealthy men endure
Were all their windows level with the faces of the Poor?
Ah! Mammon's slaves, your knees shall knock, your hearts in
terror beat,
When God demands a reason for the sorrows of the street,
    The wrong things and the bad things
    And the sad things that we meet
In the filthy lane and alley, and the cruel, heartless street.

I left the dreadful corner where the steps are never still,
And sought another window overlooking gorge and hill;
But when the night came dreary with the driving rain and sleet,
They haunted me—the shadows of those faces in the street,

Flitting by, flitting by,
Flitting by with noiseless feet,
And with cheeks that scarce were paler than the real ones in the
street.

Once I cried: "O God Almighty! if Thy might doth still endure,
Now show me in a vision for the wrongs of Earth a cure."
And, lo, with shops all shuttered I beheld a city's street,
And in the warning distance heard the tramp of many feet,
    Coming near, coming near,
    To a drum's dull distant beat,
And soon I saw the army that was marching down the street!

Then, like a swollen river that has broken bank and wall,
The human flood came pouring with the red flags over all,
And kindled eyes all blazing bright with revolution's heat,
And flashing swords reflecting rigid faces in the street—
    Pouring on, pouring on,
    To a drum's loud threatening beat,
And the war-hymns and the cheering of the people in the street.

And so it must be while the world goes rolling round its course,
The warning pen shall write in vain, the warning voice grow
hoarse,
But not until a city feels Red Revolution's feet
Shall its sad people miss awhile the terrors of the street—
    The dreadful everlasting strife
    For scarcely clothes and meat
In that pent track of living death—the city's cruel street.

To An Old Mate

Old Mate! In the gusty old weather,
When our hopes and our troubles were new,
In the years spent in wearing out leather,
I found you unselfish and true—
I have gathered these verses together
For the sake of our friendship and you.

You may think for a while, and with reason,
Though still with a kindly regret,
That I've left it full late in the season

To prove I remember you yet;
But you'll never judge me by their treason
Who profit by friends—and forget.

I remember, Old Man, I remember—
The tracks that we followed are clear—
The jovial last nights of December,
The solemn first days of the year,
Long tramps through the clearings and timber,
Short partings on platform and pier.

I can still feel the spirit that bore us,
And often the old stars will shine—
I remember the last spree in chorus
For the sake of that other Lang Syne,
When the tracks lay divided before us,
Your path through the future, and mine.

Through the frost-wind that cut like whip-lashes,
Through the ever-blind haze of the drought—
And in fancy at times by the flashes
Of light in the darkness of doubt—
I have followed the tent-poles and ashes
Of camps that we moved farther out.

You will find in these pages a trace of
That side of our past which was bright,
And recognize sometimes the face of
A friend who has dropped out of sight—
I send them along in the place of
The letters I promised to write.

Walter Withers, Australia, 1854–1914, *Fossickers*, 1893, oil on canvas 68.8 x 51 cm. Gift of Mrs L. J. de Bretteville 1969. Collection: Australian National Gallery, Canberra.

The Shearers

No church-bell rings them from the Track,
    No pulpit lights their blindness—
'Tis hardship, drought and homelessness
    That teach those Bushmen kindness:
The mateship born of barren lands,
    Oft toil and thirst and danger—
The camp-fare for the stranger set,
    The first place to the stranger.

They do the best they can to-day—
    Take no thought of the morrow;
Their way is not the old-world way—
    They live to lend and borrow.
When shearing's done and cheques gone wrong,
    They call it "time to slither"—
They saddle up and say "So-long!"
    And ride—the Lord knows whither.

And though he may be brown or black,
    Or wrong man there or right man,
The mate that's honest to his mates
    They call that man a "white man"!
They tramp in mateship side by side—
    The Protestant and "Roman"—
They call no biped lord or "sir",
    And touch their hats to no man!

They carry in their swags, perhaps,
    A portrait and a letter—
And, maybe, deep down in their hearts,
    The hope of "something better".
Where lonely miles are long to ride,
    And all days seem recurrent,
There's lots of time to think of men
    They might have been—but weren't.

They turn their faces to the west
    And leave the world behind them—
(Their drought-dried graves are seldom green
    Where even mates can find them).
They know too little of the world
    To rise to wealth or greatness:
But in this book of mine I pay
    My tribute to their straightness.

The Bush Fire

Ah, better the thud of the deadly gun, and the crash of the bursting
    shell,
Than the terrible silence where drought is fought out there in the
    western hell;
And better the rattle of rifles near, or the thunder on deck at sea,
Than the sound—most hellish of all to hear—of a fire where it should
    not be.

On the runs to the west of the Dingo Scrubs there was drought, and
    ruin, and death,
And the sandstorm came from the dread north-east with the blast of a
    furnace-breath;
Till at last one day, at the fierce sunrise, a boundary-rider woke,
And saw, in the place of the distant haze, a curtain of light blue smoke.

There is saddling-up by the cocky's hut, and out in the station yard,
And away to the north, north-east, north-west, the Bushmen are riding
    hard.
The pickets are out and many a scout, and many a mulga wire,
While Bill and Jim, with their faces grim, are riding to meet the fire.

It roars for days in the hopeless scrubs, and across, where the ground
    seems bare,
With a crackle and hiss, like the hissing of snakes, the fire is travelling
    there;
Till at last, exausted by sleeplessness, and the terrible toil and heat,
The sqatter is crying, "My God! the wool!" and the farmer, "My God!
    the wheat!"

But there comes a drunkard (who reels as he rides), with the news
    from the roadside pub:—

John Longstaff, 1862–1941, Australian, *Gippsland, Sunday night, February 20th, 1898*, oil on canvas 196.2 x 143.5 cm. National Gallery of Victoria. Purchased 1898.

"Pat Murphy—the cocky—cut off by the fire!—way back in the Dingo
    Scrub!
Let the wheat and the woolshed go to ——" Well, they do as each
    great heart bids;
They are riding a race for the Dingo Scrub—for Pat and his wife and
    kids.

And who is leading the race with Death? An ill-matched three, you'll
    allow;
Flash Jim the Breaker, and Boozing Bill (who is riding steadily now),
And Constable Dunn, of the Mounted Police, is riding between the
    two
(He wants Flash Jim, but the job can wait till they get the Murphys
    through).

As they strike the track through the blazing scrub, the trooper is heard
    to shout:
"We'll take them to the Two-mile Tank, if we cannot bring them
out!"
A half-mile more, and the rest rein back, retreating, half-choked, half-
    blind;
And the three are gone from the sight of men, and the bush fire roars
    behind.

The Bushmen wiped the tears of smoke, and like Bushmen wept and
    swore;
"Poor Bill will be wanting his drink tonight as never he did before."
"And Dunn was the best in the whole damned force!" says a client of
    Dunn's, with pride;
"I reckon he'll serve his summons on Jim—when they get to the other
    side."

It is daylight again, and the fire is past, and the black scrub silent and
    grim
Except for the blaze in an old dead tree, or the crash of a falling limb;
And the Bushmen are riding again on the run, with hearts and with eyes
    that fill,
To look for the bodies of Constable Dunn, Flash Jim, and Boozing Bill.

They are found in the mud of the Two-mile Tank where a fiend might
    scarce survive,
But the Bushmen gather from words they hear that the bodies are
    much alive.
There is Swearing Pat, with his grey beard singed, and his language of
    lurid hue,
And his tough old wife, and his half-baked kids, and the three who
    dragged them through.

Old Pat is deploring his burnt-out home, and his wife the climate warm;

And Jim the loss of his favourite horse, and Dunn of his uniform;
And Boozing Bill, with a raging thirst, is cursing the Dingo Scrub—
He'll only ask for the loan of a flask and a lift to the nearest pub.

Flash Jim the Breaker is lying low—blue-paper is after him,
And Dunn, the trooper, is riding his rounds with a blind eye out for
    Jim;
And Boozing Bill is fighting D.T.'s. in the township of Sudden Jerk—
When they're wanted again in the Dingo Scrubs, they'll be there to do
    the work.

The Old Bark School

It was built of bark and poles, and the floor was full of holes
    Where each leak in rainy weather made a pool;
And the walls were mostly cracks lined with calico and sacks—
    There was little need for windows in the school.

Then we rode to school and back by the rugged gully track,
    On the old grey horse that carried three or four;
And he looked so very wise that he lit the master's eyes
    Every time he put his head in at the door.

He had run with Cobb and Co.—"that grey leader, let him go!"
    There were men "as knowed the brand upon his hide",
And "as knowed it on the course". Funeral service: "Good old horse!"
    When we burnt him in the gully where he died.

And the master thought the same. 'Twas from Ireland that he came,
    Where the tanks are full all summer, and the feed is simply grand;
And the joker then in vogue said his lessons with a brogue—
    'Twas unconscious imitation, let the reader understand.

And we learnt the world in scraps from some ancient dingy maps
    Long discarded by the public-schools in town;
And as nearly every book dated back to Captain Cook
    Our geography was somewhat upside-down.

It was "in the book" and so—well, at that we'd let it go,
    For we never would believe that print could lie;
And we all learnt pretty soon that when we came out at noon
    "The sun is in the south part of the sky."

And Ireland! *that* was known from the coastline to Athlone:
    We got little information *re* the land that gave us birth;

Broad Street, Albury, N.S.W. (ca 1874), oil on canvas 35.5 x 51 cm. Signed either A.M.B. or A.M.G. National Library of Australia.

Save that Captain Cook was killed (and was very likely grilled)
    And "the natives of New Holland are the lowest race on earth".

And a woodcut, in its place, of the same degraded race
    Seemed a lot more like a camel than the blackfellows we knew;
Jimmy Bullock, with the rest, scratched his head and gave his best;
    But his faith was sadly shaken by a bobtailed kangaroo.

But the old bark school is gone, and the spot it stood upon
    Is a cattle-camp in winter where the curlew's cry is heard;
There's a brick school on the flat, but a schoolmate teaches that,
    For, about the time they built it, our old master was "transferred".

But the bark school comes again with exchanges 'cross the plain—
    With the *Out-Back Advertiser;* and my fancy roams at large

47

When I read of passing stock, of a western mob or flock,
    With "James Bullock", "Grey", or "Henry Dale" in charge.

And I think how Jimmy went from the old bark school content,
    With his "eddication" finished, with his pack-horse after him;
And perhaps if I were back I would take the self-same track,
    For I wish my learning ended when the Master "finished" Jim.